.CLASSICS.
Illustrated®

William Shakespeare
ROMEO and JULIET

essay by
Susan Shwartz, Ph.D.

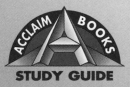

ACCLAIM BOOKS
STUDY GUIDE

Romeo and Juliet

art by George Evans

Classics Illustrated: Romeo & Juliet © Twin Circle Publishing Co.,
a division of Frawley Enterprises; licensed to First Classics, Inc.
All new material and compilation © 1996 by Acclaim Books, Inc.

Dale-Chall R.L.: 7.7

ISBN 1-57840-002-3

Acclaim Books, New York, NY
Printed in the United States

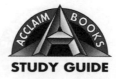

STUDY GUIDE

Romeo and Juliet

by
William Shakespeare

HUNDREDS OF YEARS AGO, IN VERONA, ITALY, TWO NOBLE FAMILIES FEUDED BITTERLY. THE TWO FAMILIES WERE THE MONTAGUES AND THE CAPULETS. EVERY MEMBER OF THE TWO HOUSEHOLDS, FROM THE SERVANTS TO THE MASTERS TOOK PART IN THE CEASELESS FIGHTING.

THE HEADS OF THE FEUDING HOUSES EACH HAD ONLY ONE CHILD. MONTAGUE HAD A SON, ROMEO. CAPULET HAD A DAUGHTER, JULIET.

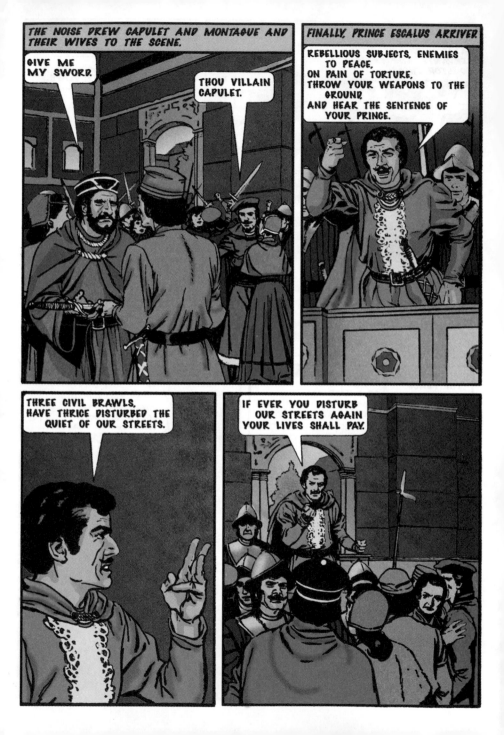

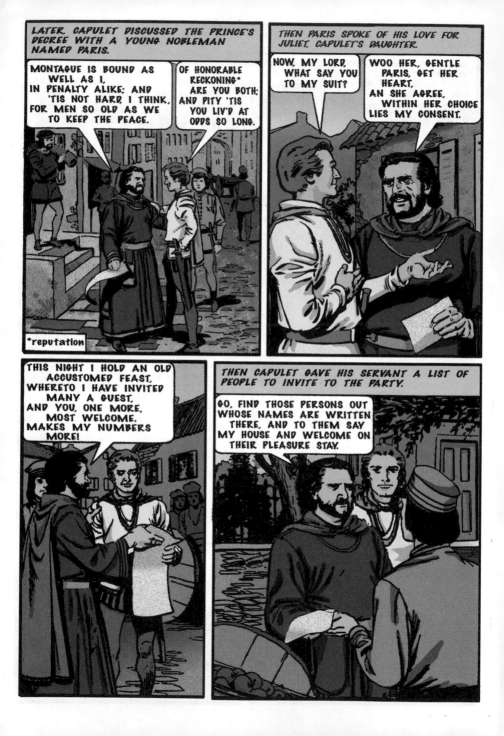

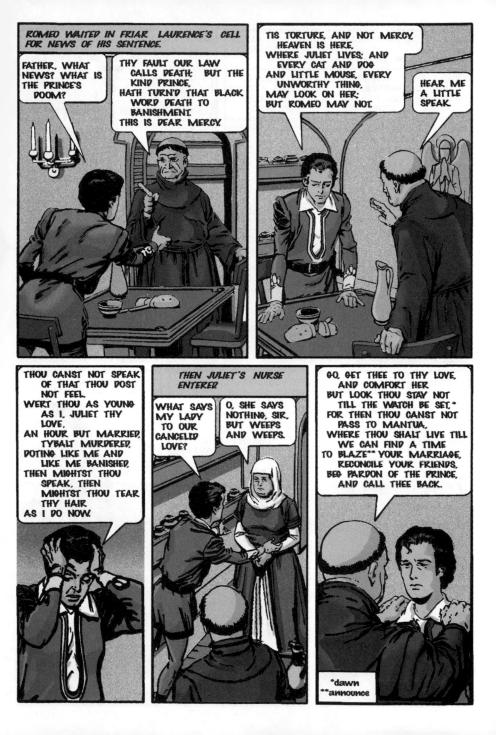

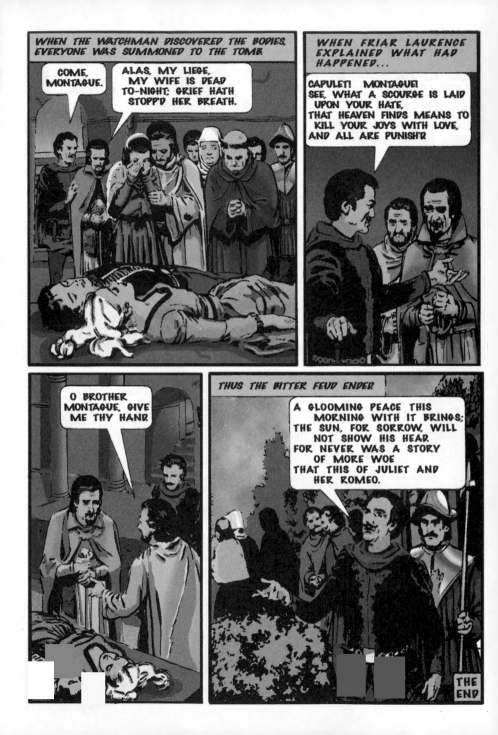

R**MEO AND JULI**T
WILLIAM SHAKESPEARE

The Author

In the current era of Shakespeare worship, in which William Shakespeare as Cultural Icon has almost crowded out Shakespeare as writer, it may take a commercial writer to point out that Shakespeare managed to achieve every writer's dream. Not only did he travel to the big city to make his fortune, he worked at what he loved, succeeded at it financially, in the praise of his audience, and the respect of his colleagues. He rose in the world and retired, a well-off man, back to his home town.

Although Shakespeare's sonnets speak about the immortality of poetry, his own writing — far from being engraved in stone or cast in bronze — was meant to be participated in. It requires the contribution of actors, a director, and a living, feeling audience to make it whole. Like any dramatic work, it is fluid — an actor or director can take it, set it in a different period, or alter it by different emphases — called "readings" in the theatre and lit-crit businesses — of particularly problematic lines. And every reader can take something away that belongs simultaneously to the world and to the individual.

In Shakespeare's case, scholars, directors, and performers have wrangled about his texts for centuries. For performances, his plays can and have been cut, one version of a line selected over another, and — sometimes — even the endings changed. Imagine, for example, a *Romeo and Juliet* or a *King Lear* with a happy ending. It's been done. As Shakespeare himself says in Hamlet, "Oh, there has been a great throwing about of brains." Some people have even denied that Shakespeare wrote his own work and attributed the plays to other people, usually more elaborately educated and nobly born types like Sir Francis Bacon. There's even a rather engaging mystery — and curse — on Shakespeare's grave in Stratford-on-Avon, his home.

But let's look at the writer who lived in rooms in London, owned shares in a prominent theatre, managed to get himself in trouble in the country before traveling to London where political trouble sometimes found him, who didn't find a lawsuit or two at all amiss, and who wrote plays that have managed to enter the English language as classics, often produced and quoted so often that you may not even be aware you're quoting Shakespeare.

The parish church of Holy Trinity records the baptism on April 26, 1564, of William Shakespeare in Stratford-upon-Avon, in Warwickshire, some 85 miles northwest of London.

No record of his birth survives, although it's usually celebrated on April 23 because that is the day of England's patron Saint George — and of Shakespeare's death in 1616.

His father John, born to tenant farmers, was an ambitious man. In an age of expansion, he rose to own his own glover's shop and to become Bailiff of Stratford, a position similar to mayor. He married a Mary Arden, of slightly better birth than he and an heiress, and bought two houses. In around 1576, he applied to the Office of Heralds for the right to be called gentleman; this meant, among other things, that he would be granted a coat of arms. Although this petition went nowhere at the time because of what sounds like a bad run of financial and political luck, William Shakespeare subsequently saw his father's dream through. It is reflected in his writing; *The Winter's Tale*, one of his very last plays, has a funny scene in which a clown and a shepherd joke about being "gentlemen born," albeit only for four hours so far.

Shakepeare grew up as the eldest child, with three younger brothers and two younger sisters, a solidly middle-class family in an unwalled medieval town. As befitted solid citizens during Elizabeth's reign, the Shakespeares were members of the Church of England, and lived through the wars against Spain (they would have been part of the nation-wide rejoicing when the Spanish Armada was destroyed in 1588, for example). He attended the Stratford grammar school, where he chiefly learned Latin — so much for "little Latin and less Greek" — but not Oxford or Cambridge University like other leading playwrights of his day like Ben Jonson.

He probably learned as much from his surroundings — the forests, the River Avon, market days, and a fair for which Stratford was famous in the region.

A mercantile town, it drew companies of actors that put on performances at the guild-hall. By the time Shakespeare was a youth, he had probably seen plays put on by the Earl of Warwick's men, the Earl of Worcester's men, and England's leading adult company, whose patron was the Earl of Leicester and whose principal artist was the James Burbage who built the first theatre in London and became the father of the great actor Richard Burbage, Shakespeare's colleague and friend.

William Shakespeare married young, in 1582, to Anne Hathaway of Stratford, who was eight years older than he and who gave birth to his eldest child Susanna on May 26, 1583. William and Anne had two other children, twins--Judith and Hamnet, baptized February 2, 1585.

By 1592, as demonstrated by a performance of *Henry VI*, Shakespeare had moved to London to make his fortune as actor, playwright, and share owner in a theatrical company.

Many writers who move to the big city are told "don't give up the day job." Shakespeare's day job was the thing he loved. He made a considerable impression early on and drew the fire of less-successful literary men such as Robert Greene, who complained about an "upstart crow...with a Tiger's heart wrapped in a player's hide.."

ROMEO AND JULIET
TOGETHER AT LAST IN CYBERSPACE

William Shakespeare and his plays are alive and well on the WorldWide Web. In addition to various Usenet groups where the plays and their author can be discussed at length with people from all over the world, a quick search of the World Wide Web turned up the following (as of September, 1996):

• **70,972** matches containing the word "Shakespeare" and including everything from textual scholarship to university libraries to a Klingon translation of *Hamlet* (with a great graphic of a Klingon in a doublet) to individual theatre companies and productions and how Shakespeare can be taught in the schools. As a starting point for your explorations, try the Shakespeare home page: **http://www.shakespeare.com/**

• A search on the name "Romeo" turned up about **20,000** matches, most of them having to do with sports cars, designer clothing, and the occasional namesake, but the remainder dealing with Shakespeare's play or spin-offs.

• The search on "Juliet, " produced more than **10,000** mentions. In addition to various women of that name (including scientists, film and music fans), Massachusetts Institute of Technology maintains the main page for discussion of Shakespeare's play at: **http://the-tech.mit/edu/Shakespeare/ cgibin/commentary/get/Tragedy/ Romeoandjuliet/romeoandjuliet/ HTML/**

(It may be easier to click on MIT's Web page and navigate from there!)

• Want to write to Juliet for advice on your love life? The "Club di Giulietta" was founded in 1972 by writers and artists, and each year, on Valentine's Day, it awards a prize for the best love letter; it lists an address for Juliet at:
giulietta@easy1.easynet it
For those who would rather write her the old-fashioned way:
Club di Giulietta-Imaggine di Verona
Via Galilei n.3, 37100 Verona – Italia
Juliet has received and answered letters advising people from all over the world. Elvis Costello has even written a song about these letters.

• You can also use the Web to "travel" to Verona and tour houses in that ancient walled city — from Juliet's balcony to Juliet's tomb — without leaving your keyboard. Or, you can look at Juliet, the sixth known satellite of the planet Uranus, discovered in 1986 by Voyager 2, and remember Juliet's line "and when he shall die/Take him and cut him out in little stars,/And he will make the face of heaven so fine/That all the world will be in love with night/And pay no worship to the garish sun."

who dared to believe himself the only "Shake-scene" in the country. Such writers resented not only his popularity, but his lack of a university degree.

In London, Shakespeare was able to live in a city much larger than his native Stratford. Elizabeth's London was, above all things, *alive* — a city filled with history, turmoil, and politics. No doubt, between performances and writing marathons, Shakespeare had a chance to talk with soldiers and sailors, actors, and nobles. No doubt he stayed up nights in taverns drinking (how else could he have created Falstaff?), hearing old battle stories and new stories of the New World, all of which went into his plays. No doubt, he saw the heads of traitors exhibited on London Bridge.

But Shakespeare didn't just listen to the rough-and-tumble crowd. Like his father, he had an eye to advancement, which meant important patrons. By 1594, Shakespeare had also become distinguished as a poet — elaborate, sophisticated verse that won him the praise of young noblemen — as well as a playwright.

His output is relatively small — some 37 plays plus several, like *Two Noble Kinsmen*, that are collaborations — plus his sonnet cycle and several long, secular poems. But he prospered from them and became well known. *Merry Wives of Windsor* was written in obedience to Queen Elizabeth, who wanted to see "Falstaff in Love." A Queen's notice could be tricky, however: a production of *Richard II* could very easily have backfired upon him because it dealt with the overthrow of a king.

In 1596, Shakespeare's son Hamnet died. Also in that year, and ironically enough, Shakespeare achieved his father's dream of a coat of arms: he was a gentleman, now, but without an heir. Nevertheless, he kept on. In 1599, he was listed as a shareholder in the newly constructed Globe Theatre and arguably the most popular playwright in the City. In 1603, Queen Elizabeth died, and King James I ultimately took over Shakespeare's company, which became known as the King's Men. From 1598 to 1609, he wrote some of his finest plays, among them *As You Like It, Henry V, Julius Caesar, Much Ado About Nothing, Hamlet, Othello*, and

many others. (*Romeo and Juliet* dates from 1591.)

No doubt Shakespeare divided his time between London and Stratford, where he retired and where he died in 1616. He was buried as "Will. Shakspere, gent." (probably to his satisfaction, if only he could see it) and buried within the parish church, with a rhyme on his headstone cursing anyone who disturbed his bones — which have, as a matter of fact, never been touched.

He lived to see his grandchildren and to be acclaimed as a playwright and as a gentleman. In 1623, old friends and actors John Heminge and Henry Condell cooperated with the London stationers in publishing a collected edition of his plays, complete with picture and an ode by the poet and playwright Ben Jonson, who hailed him as "not of an age, but for all time."

Jonson never wrote a better line.

Before we turn to the actual story, we should probably pay some attention to the tradition in which Shakespeare worked. He lived in a time when he would have heard traditional ballads such as those of Robin Hood, when the stories of King Arthur were falling into disfavor because of disapproval by scholars of the New Learning, and when people enjoyed listening to "sad stories of the deaths of kings." For them, Richard II and Richard III, or Henry V, were not just monarchs: they were stories. And for a playwright who had to write fast to provide his company — and the rowdy and demanding Elizabethan audiences (to say nothing of Her Majesty herself) — with fresh material, Shakespeare learned early on to borrow where he could. While it's fairly obvious where he got the material for his history plays, he drew *King Lear* from Geoffrey of Monmouth's *History of the Kings of Britain* (a source for stories of Arthur), *Hamlet* from another popular history, and *Macbeth* from a far earlier one. He drew *Troilus and Cressida* from Greek epic as it was transformed during the Middle Ages by poets such as Geoffrey Chaucer — and *The Tempest*, at least partially, from a shipwreck on Bermuda during the English exploration of the New World. Who knows? Perhaps he even saw a native American brought to the Old World from the New.

For *Romeo and Juliet*, Shakespeare's source was *The Tragicall Historye of Romeus and Iuliet written first in Italian by Bandell, and now in English by Ar. Br.* (Arthur Brooke, 1562). Brooke's source was a long poem based on the prose of the Italian writer Bandello (1554) through a 1559 French version. The story wasn't original to Bandello either:

DRAMATIS PERSONAE

The fact that you'll often see in an edition of one of Shakespeare's plays the term "Dramatis Personae" should indicate to you the bookish nature — to some extent — of the Elizabethan playwrights. Shakespeare himself fell afoul of some of them because he was not university-educated. For the Elizabethans, what a university education meant is very different from what it means to us. The university in the sixteenth and seventeenth centuries was very different, as well, from its medieval roots. It still stressed the seven liberal arts, which were divided into two branches: the Trivium (grammar, rhetoric and logic) and the Quadrivium (arithmetic, music, geometry and astronomy). It still had a strong theological component. It lacked, of course, the technological and business disciplines that we have come to expect in universities. And much of the reading and the lectures were in Latin, which was considered the preeminent language of scholarly discourse. One of the things that made something "popular" rather than scholarly, in fact, was the fact that it was written in English, rather than in Latin. Students would act out plays in Latin and Greek: university-educated men, upon leaving (or, as they said, "going down from university") their universities, carried their taste for plays into later life.

Luigi da Porto used it in 1525 and Masuccio Salernitano in 1476. Some of the people who watched the play on its opening night (probably some time around 1591) might have known some of these stories: many cultivated Englishmen and women read and spoke and sang Italian. For them, the question wasn't: *what* happens next, but *how* is it going to happen?

If Shakespeare didn't have the job of making up the story, he faced a very different challenge:

SEEING A SHOW, ELIZABETHAN STYLE

Theatre-going in Shakespeare's time wasn't the high-brow activity we may consider it today. Everyone went, from the lowest-born to the most noble. The "cheap seats" then were what we call the Orchestra Section nowadays—the area directly surrounding the stage, which stuck right out into the audience area. Shakespeare's theatre, The Globe, had no roof (which meant that plays were performed during the day, and in good weather, or not at all), and were usually built in a circle or octagon, with several tiers of balconies facing the stage. There was seating in the balconies, but the groundlings—the folks in the cheap seats—had to stand up...or sit on the edge of the stage. You brought your lunch to the play, maybe bought some ale or a pastry from a seller (who might be strolling through the theatre, yelling like a hot-dog vendor at a baseball game) and watched the show—or didn't. Groundlings talked to, yelled at, even got into fights with the players!

There were no curtains to hide stagehands while sets were changed (or actors hiding from wrathful groundlings!) and in fact very few sets were used. When the Chorus (a sort of on-stage narrator) speaks in prologue of "Fair Verona, where we set our scene," or tells the audience

"Think, when we talk of horses, that you see them
Printing their proud hoofs i' the receiving earth.
For 'tis your thoughts that now must deck our kings
Carry them here and there, jumping o'er times..."

at the beginning of Shakespeare's history play *Henry V*, it was acknowledging that audience's imagination regularly supplied the settings the theatre itself could not.

Interior of the Swan Theatre.
From a drawing by Johannrs de Witt (1596).

making it his own. Thus, he makes a variety of choices — just as writers do today. He shortens how long the story takes to go from meeting to tragedy from nine months to less than a week. He makes Mercutio a major character quite capable of stopping the show with his poetry. To add interest to actions on stage, he provides several duels with Tybalt, Prince of Cats. He makes the Nurse a warm, comic, and robust figure, not at all averse to a dirty joke. Very subtly, he manages to make us aware

how very different Romeo's family the Montagues are from Juliet's somewhat trying family, the Capulets. He mixes comedy and tragedy so that the reader — or the audience — laughs through tears as Mercutio puns after he's taken his death wound, then shudders as he curses "both your houses" — the Capulets and the Montagues.

Probably Shakespeare's most inspired choice was making Romeo and Juliet little more than children: his sources make Juliet around 18, not almost 14 as she is in the play. Their sudden kindling into love, and the growth of that love into a passion bigger than they and heartbreakingly unselfish and mature, is part of their tragedy: they loved so well, yet had such a short time to live.

Plot

The play begins with a prologue setting the place (Verona), the problem (an "ancient grudge") and the tragedy ("a pair of star-crossed lovers" who take their lives). After the formality of the prologue, Shakespeare shifts quickly to a street scene that turns into a brawl. "Do you bite your thumb, sir?" refers to a vulgar gesture that has its analog in modern-day disrespectful actions. These are fighting words, and a fight is what they provoke. A good production of the play (or the ballet) fills the stage with what looks like a highly enjoyable brawl. These people are young, with more energy than they know what to do with. Of course, they're going to get into trouble.

And of course they do. Instantly. Into this brawl comes Prince Escalus, ruler of Verona, who is sick of the whole feud between the Montagues and the Capulets. The next person, he vows, to break the peace will pay for it with his life. He plans to administer what sounds like one of a series of reprimands to the heads of each house. Lord Montague is left behind, asking his nephew where his son is. It's a good question:

Romeo is in love with Rosaline, and his love takes the form of chivalrous, sentimental moping that amuses everyone except for him — and doesn't make Rosaline think well of him at all.

Meanwhile, Lord Capulet and Count Paris are discussing Paris's proposal to marry Juliet, who is almost 14 — a little young for marriage, her father thinks

(he married an even younger woman, and it hasn't turned out particularly well), but Capulet is a soft touch: he agrees that Paris can try to win her love if he can. He is more interested in planning an elaborate party and sends out a servant with a list of guests. **(Act 1 Scene 2)** The servant, who is illiterate, finds someone to read the list to him and — as luck (luck plays a significant role in the play) would have it, he happens upon Benvolio and Romeo, who decide it would be fun to put on masks and crash their enemy's party.

Meanwhile, Juliet is preparing for the ball and for the rest of her life, as her mother and her nurse joke with her and tell her about Count Paris's proposal. It hardly seems real to her.

Romeo, Benvolio, and their friend Mercutio do indeed intrude on Capulet's party, where Romeo meets Juliet and instantly ("oh, she doth teach the torches to burn bright") falls in love **(Act 1 Scene 5)**.

Juliet's cousin, Tybalt, a very fiery young man, is infuriated that Romeo is at the party. Only Lord Capulet's direct command stops him from challenging him right then and there. Romeo and Juliet, already in love over their heads, each ask who the other is. "My only love sprung from my only hate!" Juliet laments. Therein lies the tragedy.

After the party ends, neither Romeo nor Juliet can rest. Romeo climbs the wall of her house and sees her standing at her balcony — a famous scene that is one of the classic roles for any actress **(Act 2, Scene 2)**.

They declare their love for each other and make plans to marry. The ceremony will be performed by Friar Laurence, who is spiritual advisor and confessor to both of them, who is an expert with herbs, and who sees in the two young people's love a chance to end the feud that has been wrecking Verona's peace.

While Romeo and Juliet are being married, Tybalt, Juliet's cousin, encounters Romeo's kinsmen Mercutio and Benvolio **(Act 3 Scene 1)**.

He challenges them to a fight even though Escalus has declared brawling a capital offense. The fight is proceeding very entertainingly when Romeo approaches and tries to stop it — just in time

for Tybalt to give Mercutio a mortal wound he might not have had if Romeo hadn't gotten in the way. In a fury of grief and anger, Romeo kills Tybalt.

Juliet, waiting for her brand-new husband, realizes that he has killed her beloved cousin and that he must leave the city the next day or be executed. As if that's not bad enough, her father decides that what she needs to be happy again is a young husband — Count Paris. Although she protests, he and Lady Capulet, Juliet's mother, scold her: if she disobeys them, they wish her dead. She runs to Friar Laurence, who helps her devise a desperate plan: he will give her a potion that will make her seem dead **(Act 4 Scene 1)**. She will be "buried" in her family tomb, and Friar Laurence will rescue her and see her reunited with Romeo. Has she courage enough to try?

She has. Unfortunately, she *is* a "star-crossed" lover. Laurence's message to Romeo goes astray, although a different messenger does manage to tell Romeo of Juliet's death **(Act 5 Scene 1)**. He resolves to go back to Verona, take poison, and die at her side.

He enters the tomb and finds Count Paris mourning. Of course, he kills the count; sees Juliet on her bier, and swallows the poison — only moments before the potion she has swallowed wears off and she wakes **(Act 5 Scene 3)**. Friar Laurence tries to hustle her

away from where her husband lies dead, but Juliet sees him. When the Friar goes away, she mourns that Romeo has drunk all the poison, then takes his dagger and stabs herself.

Prince Escalus has the last words: "See what a scourge is laid upon your hate... All are punished." And he closes the play just as the prologue began it:

*"For never was a
story of more woe
Than this of Juliet and
her Romeo."*

Let's begin with the characters of *Romeo and Juliet* by dividing them into three categories: the Montagues; the Capulets; and Verona.

The Montagues
Lord Montague — He seems older and graver than Lord Capulet. A dignified man with a wife who backs him (and who dies of sorrow), he is less inclined to arranging festivals and less temperamental than Lord Capulet. He has raised a son whose reputation in Verona is high, and he listens to, as well as orders, his younger kinsmen.

Benvolio — A cousin to Romeo (rather than the Montague heir), Benvolio is a good-natured youth. His name is taken from Italian words that mean "well-wishing." He is even-tempered (except in the matter of street fights), loyal to Romeo and able to joke and tease him.

Mercutio — Also of the house of Montague, Mercutio is a much different personality than anyone else in it — or in the play. His name derives from "Mercury." As befits someone with that name, he is mercurial — quick-tempered, fast to change moods, spirited, and a master of verbal by-play: puns, jokes, witticisms, and insults. He moves fast and is a fine fencer, with the type of pride that one would expect of a member of the minor nobility.

Romeo — Heir to the house of Montague, Romeo is described even by Lord Capulet as a "well-governed youth." He opens the play as the stereotypical despairing lover whom his friends tease.

His father is aware of this, yet seems well-relieved to have him out of the fighting. He allows himself to be persuaded to go to the ball at the Capulets more to indulge his friends and because Rosaline, his unattainable lady, will be present. When he sees Juliet, however, he falls instantly in love and his entire personality seems to change. His language kindles into poetry and passion. It is full of metaphor and is both loving and respectful; from it, you can tell how quickly and completely he has been enchanted. His meeting with Juliet beneath her balcony shows him to have a poet's soul, coupled with the impulsiveness of a very young man who is very much in love. He has courage, but he also has some of the volatility of his friend and kinsman Mercutio: his confessor condemns him for emotionalism. After his marriage, he is filled with goodwill, which extends as far as Juliet's kinsman Tybalt. He tries to make peace, and his friend Mercutio dies as a result. Because of his impulsive rage, he kills Tybalt and; later, when he hears of Juliet's "death," he takes his own life.

JULIET TOLD HER FATHER SHE WOULD NOT MARRY PARIS.

DISOBEDIENT WRETCH! GET THEE TO CHURCH O' THURSDAY, OR NEVER AFTER LOOK ME IN THE FACE.

The Capulets
Lord Capulet — Much older than his wife, he is a proud man who insists on being master in his own house. When he is challenged, he flies into a rage; insulting Tybalt and commanding him to obey him, wishing Juliet dead. It is easy to see why his wife yields to his wishes.

Yet, he has a more jovial side. He loves to give parties and will sit and reminisce with the other older men. By his own lights he means well to Count Paris. His temper is quick, but it dies down quickly too; after Romeo and Juliet's death, he calls Montague "brother" and seeks reconciliation.

Lady Capulet — She tells Juliet that when she was her daughter's age, she already had a child. Married to a much older man, she is guided by him to the point where she turns on her only child and wishes her dead. Like her husband, she has a temper that flashes on and off. Her first appearance is as a loving mother. She grieves passionately (perhaps too much so) at Tybalt's death, and even more when she thinks that Juliet is dead. She seems somewhat embittered and ruled by her emotions.

The Nurse — One of Shakespeare's great comic characters. She is old, nearly toothless, but she remembers a long and well-filled life – sometimes at overly great length. She loves to laugh and will tell bawdy jokes, (shocking Juliet and dismaying Lady Capulet). She is well able to banter with the young Montagues and can trade jokes with the best of them. She sincerely loves Juliet and wishes her well: but "well" for the nurse is a "happy ever after" of marriage and babies that may not include Juliet's true love. This shows when she advises Juliet to marry Count Paris, even though she is already married — a cynicism that revolts Juliet and causes her to take desperate action.

THEN HIE YOU HENCE TO FRIAR LAURENCE' CELL; THERE STAYS A HUSBAND TO MAKE YOU A WIFE.

READING SHAKESPEARE'S VERSE

Reading Shakespearean verse is one time when it's okay to move your lips as you read. Shakespeare meant his lines to be spoken, and it's often by hearing, rather than reading, the words, that their true music and meaning come out. Almost all of Shakespeare's plays were written in blank (unrhymed) iambic pentameter. That means each line is made up of five "feet" with a particular kind of rhythm; in the case of an iamb, the rhythm of the foot is **ba-BAH**.

Thus, Romeo says to Juliet:

*If **I** profane with **my** unworthiest hand*
*This **holy shrine**, the **gentle fine** is **this**:*
*My **lips**, two **blushing pilgrims**, ready **stand***
*To **smooth** that **rough** touch with a **tender kiss**.*

It's interesting to know that when you hear a rhyme, it may have been a cue for stage-hands and cast members off stage to be ready someone's entrance, or for a scene change!

Tybalt — The young Montagues joke about Tybalt as "prince of cats" because he is a notable duellist and hothead. This proves to be everyone's downfall. Much-loved among the Capulets, he is haughty and quick to anger in a family grudge. Obviously, Juliet adores her splendid older cousin to such an extent that her father thinks that only marriage will dry her tears.

Count Paris — A suitor to Juliet, he is handsome and rich. Clearly, he is in love with her far more deeply than, say, Romeo loved Rosaline. He goes to her tomb to grieve, but jumps to the worst possible conclusion at Romeo's presence. In his actions and his temperament, he seems like the Renaissance nobleman that he is.

Juliet — In the course of the play, Juliet grows from an innocent girl to a passionate and loyal woman capable of deep love and sacrifice. She starts by trusting the people about her. She is willing to be guided by her parents and her nurse. But when she meets Romeo at the ball at her house, her path is permanently changed. After her own fashion, she is quite witty, well able to match Romeo's witticisms about pilgrims and quick to tell him when he asks what he should swear by that he should not swear at all, let alone by the moon, which waxes and wanes. Or, she adds, if he must swear an oath, let him swear it by himself.: she seems to know, instinctively, that she has chosen a lover who will be true to her. "My only love sprung from my only hate" shows that Juliet has a perfect understanding of her situation: unfortunately, her judgment and her circumstances work against her. Even in the worst possible situations, however, her loyalty, courage, and love shine through.

O, SWEAR NOT BY THE MOON, TH' INCONSTANT MOON, THAT MONTHLY CHANGES IN HER CIRCLED ORB, LEST THAT THY LOVE PROVE LIKEWISE VARIABLE.

Verona — Escalus, Friar Laurence, and the street scene

Escalus — Prince Escalus of Verona is clearly at his wits' end, confronted with a family feud that disrupts his city on a daily basis. Because he is angry at the feud — and the disobedience to his commands that it entails — he makes a hasty and extreme judgment: anyone else breaking the peace will be executed. Although he modifies it in Romeo's case enough to allow him to go into exile, he is not a man who is used to having his will disregarded. In Escalus, authority and a kind of sensitivity go hand in hand. He is used to command, used to rule, but capable of being deeply touched, as shows when he ends the play by saying that both Montague and Capulet have been punished by what they love the most.

Friar Lawrence — He is confessor, or spiritual advisor, to both Romeo and Juliet. A "friar" or follower of the brothers of St. Francis of Assisi, he is a gentle man who loves his garden, is skilled in herbcraft, and genuinely concerned for the welfare of Romeo and Juliet. He also very much wants peace in Verona and sees in their love a way of ending the feud that has divided the city. Although he gives Romeo good advice about self-control, he himself proves lacking in nerve when he tries to spirit Juliet away at the end of the play — another of the adults who fails the young lovers.

The Street Scene — The minor characters in the play reflect the mood of the play. They are quick to brawl, quick to take offense, a crowd of people who are swayed by the least thing. That's their weakness. Their strength is their immense vitality, which can bring life to the street scenes when the play is produced.

One reason a play like *Romeo and Juliet* is considered a classic is that, over the course of time, people realize that it has become a part of their own lives and their own hearts. To put it simply: the play says things that we've felt, are feeling, or perhaps wish we could feel better than we can. Like all great art, it makes us feel more keenly than, perhaps, we can bear to for very long.

If you take the story apart, there isn't all that much to it. For one thing, Shakespeare borrows an old story. For another, doesn't it deal with things we're familiar with? Two young people in love, despite their parents' disapproval; a brawl or so; a feud that divides a town in half; tragic accidents to people too young and too passionate to think? We *know* all that. Those of us still in our teens think of Romeo and Juliet and how they loved each other, and cling a little more closely to our boy- or girlfriends. Those of us who are older are grateful, perhaps, not to be "passion's slave" (as Hamlet would say), relieved not to be at the mercy of parents, prince, and fate — but still, we sigh, remembering the first time we cared that much. If we've never cared that much, as we watch the play or read it, we regret it. Just for a moment out of our practical, well-organized lives, we may even feel as if we too would count the world well lost for love.

Maybe we all do know better. Maybe we all have more common sense. But even if you do not look closely, you can see why the lovers chose as they did. They are such very fine young people. Even Lord Capulet, who has no reason to love his enemy's heir, speaks in a complimentary way of Romeo. He and Juliet are not just very attractive children on the threshold of adulthood: they are honorable, brave, and true; and they love with all their hearts.

ROMEO WAITED FOR AN OPPORTUNITY TO SPEAK TO JULIET AT LAST...

IF I PROFANE WITH MY UNWORTHIEST HAND THIS HOLY SHRINE, THE GENTLE FINE IS THIS: MY LIPS, TWO BLUSHING PILGRIMS, READY STAND TO SMOOTH THAT ROUGH TOUCH WITH A TENDER KISS.

GOOD PILGRIM, YOU DO WRONG YOUR HAND TOO MUCH.

Their love ennobles them and makes them brave — too brave, unfortunately; and their tragic courage heals the rift between their houses.

Elizabethan English, the mighty iambic pentameter line of the sixteenth and seventeenth centuries, is difficult reading for us at the very end of the twentieth century. We do not know all the words, and, if we're to feel what the writer wants us to, there really isn't time to look them up.

Someone going to a Shakespearean play for the first time would do better to forget the vocabulary lists (save that for class). Instead, simply follow the story, listen for the feelings — which a well-trained actor is well able to convey — and listen for the language patterns that you *will* find in the play if you give it half a chance.

For example, look at the images of stars and fire, from "Oh she doth teach the torches to burn bright" to the balcony scene into which dawn intrudes,

SPEAKING SHAKESPEARE

Shakespeare's plays have been around for so long (400+ years) and have been so widely quoted, so often, that his language has become a part of our own. Here are some well known lines from *Romeo and Juliet* and some phrases you might not have known were Shakespeare at all!

A pair of star-crossed lovers...
[Chorus, Prologue, Act. I line 6]

...sad hours seem long.
[Romeo, Act I, Scene I, line 164]

I will make thee think thy swan a crow.
[Benvolio, Act I, Sc. II, line 92]

O, she doth teach the torches to burn bright!
It seems she hangs upon the cheek of night
Like a bright jewel in an Ethiop's ear...
[Romeo, Act I, Sc. V, lines 45-47]

You kiss by the book.
[Juliet, Act I, Sc. V, line 116]

My only love, sprung from my only hate!
Too early seen unknown, and known too late!
[Juliet, Act I, Sc. V, lines 147-48]

He jests at scars that never felt a wound.
But soft! What light through yonder window breaks?
[Romeo, Act II, Sc. II, lines 1-2]

O, Romeo, Romeo! Wherefore art thou Romeo?
[Juliet, Act II, Sc. II, line 35]

What's in a name? That which we call a rose

By any other name would smell as sweet.
[Juliet, Act II, Sc. II, lines 45-46]

O, swear not by the moon, th' inconstant moon,
That monthly changes in her circled orb,
Lest that thy love prove likewise variable.
[Juliet, Act II, Sc. II, lines 114-16]

Good night, good night! Parting is such sweet sorrow
That I shall say good night till it be morrow.
[Juliet, Act II, Sc. II, lines 200-1]

A plague o' both your houses.
[Mercutio, Act III, Sc. I, line 90]

... 'tis not so deep as a well nor so wide as a church door;
but 'tis enough, 'twill serve.
[Mercutio, Act III, Sc. I, lines 96-97]

Thank me no thankings, nor proud me no prouds...
[Lord Capulet, Act III, Scene V, line 157]

Death, that hath sucked the honey of thy breath,
Hath had no power yet upon thy beauty.
[Romeo, Act V, Sc. III, lines 92-93]

For never was a story of more woe
Than that of Juliet and her Romeo.
[Prince, Act. V, Sc. III, lines 323-24]

to Juliet's wish that Romeo, after his death, should be cut up and set, in the form of little stars into the night sky, to make people prefer the night to the moon. Look at the opposition of night, which is for lovers, and dawn/daytime, when lovers must part, in the balcony scene and then again after Romeo and Juliet's wedding night. Or, if you want a more ominous chain of images, try to count how many times someone in Juliet's family speaks of her in connection with the dead, or wishes her dead. Even the language helps the story along and becomes, after years, a part of the people who hear it so that, when they have a need, they can borrow it to express emotions of their own. Shakespeare's plays, as the tired old joke says, are full of quotations.

Over the past four centuries, Romeo and Juliet have become synonymous with the star-crossed lovers of their prologue — from the sad teenagers in the school five towns over who drowned themselves because their parents wouldn't let them date, to the tragic duo, one Christian, one Muslim, shot in Bosnia and left to lie there until the world took pity on them, to anyone who's ever loved the wrong person because of age, wealth, race, or simple parental dislike. They exist in many different forms and pose a lasting challenge not only for audiences but for artists.

Leonard Bernstein transformed the two lovers into New Yorkers and gang members — Puerto Rican and Anglo — in *West Side Story*. Composers from Gounod to Prokofiev to Tschaikovsky to Elvis Costello have attempted to set their story to music. Every girl who has wanted to dance or act has tried to portray Juliet, and every boy who has fallen in love and made a bit of a fool, or a swaggering nuisance of himself has been called "Romeo." The roles are a test for actors and actresses, and company after theatre company puts the play on year after year. Film versions exist — from the elaborate Zeffirelli *Romeo and Juliet* (available on videotape) with Olivia Hussey and Leonard Whiting, to the great ballet film, with Shakespeare's words replaced astonishingly well by music and dance, starring Rudolf Nureyev and Margot Fonteyn. The most recent film adaptation, starring Leonardo DiCaprio and Claire Danes, is set in modern times.

All this artistry and tradition notwithstanding, what we as individual readers or spectators take away from the play is the brief, passionate love of two people who are little more than children. Their story flares across our minds and hearts like a comet. A few decades ago Juliet's 13 years seemed a preposterous age at which to have a child. Yet today, many young girls do have children; when you look at Lady Capulet, you see that it really isn't the best idea in the world (even though Lady Capulet's husband is well able to support his family).

Something has gone out of the Lady's life — a carefree youth, maybe? She is bitter, too quick to support her husband against her child, too quick to wish her daughter dead, too quick to mourn passionately at Tybalt's death (one rather common reading in the play and in the ballet is to make her and Tybalt seem to be lovers), and too quick to wish herself dead too.

Romeo and Juliet is also a play in which, with the best will in the world, things get out of hand so quickly and so completely that you really do believe that Fate has taken some malignant interest. Terrible coincidences occur. Romeo intervenes in Mercutio's and Tybalt's duel just in time to get Mercutio killed. The Friar's letter to Romeo goes undelivered; the messenger telling Romeo his wife Juliet is dead manages to find him — and he dies of it. Juliet wakes one moment too late. Mercutio, one of Shakespeare's wittiest and attractive minor characters, dies in broad daylight, his jokes turned to pain. In the Zeffirelli film, as he's dying, his friends laugh. They don't believe it's real, but he knows better and screams in anger, cursing, as he tries to make them understand.

"Of all the words of tongue or pen," runs the cliché, "the saddest are 'it might have been.'" *Romeo and Juliet* is a play full of "might have beens."

And would it have been so bad if the "might have beens" had happened? you may think.

AS ROMEO FLED A CROWD GATHERED AT THE SCENE OF THE FIGHT.

TYBALT! O MY BROTHER'S CHILD!

BENVOLIO, WHO BEGAN THIS BLOODY FRAY?

You wouldn't be wrong or a cultural illiterate, if, instead of analyzing the image patterns, the sources, the various themes of the play, you turn to the characters themselves as if they are people you know and love. In some sense, of course, they are.

Would you have tried to talk sense into Tybalt? Would you have reasoned with Prince Escalus? Could you have comforted Juliet, perhaps, or tried to calm Romeo in his first frantic grief? If only they had known! If only you could have told them...

...But you can't — and therein lies another aspect of the tragedy. You see these people rushing headlong toward their deaths, and you cannot stop them. Despite the terrible productions in which Juliet woke up in time, you would not wish things otherwise — even if you do leave the theatre with red eyes.

In their desire to choose for themselves and love for themselves, Romeo and Juliet seem very much like ourselves. But medieval doctrine about love (they had books full of it) taught that true love brings out the best that is in us; and the two lovers prove the truth of that.

They are children at the beginning of the play. Romeo droops after a woman who scorns him, more in love, it seems, with the idea of love than with an actual woman: any woman pretty enough and distant enough might do to attract him. Juliet is still a child, deferential with her mother, playful with her nurse, more than a little surprised at the idea that she would be considered for the "honor" of marriage.

They no sooner see each other than they fall in love, hard and fast. Shakespeare's language is fine enough that you get the splendid poetry; you get the spectacle; you get the music and costumes and dances that have always accompanied the play. But you also get the feelings: these are impetuous, hot-blooded people for whom, quite literally, there will be no tomorrow.

Is their tragic death a waste of the years they might have had? If you count only in years, certainly. If you count in terms of depths of feeling, in terms of the effect they've had on countless thousands of watchers, it's hard to agree. And, all in all, is their tragedy really such a waste?

Like the fires and stars they speak in terms of, all things die; all things pass; and at least they have a moment of total joy. It is impossible to think of them as growing older, worrying about taxes, or how to marry off children of their own: they remain forever young in our hearts.

There are, perhaps, worse things, we may think as we sit comfortably in the theatre or lounge at home on our sofa watching the movie on the VCR. For a moment, we become onlookers in Verona. And then, we return, a little teary around the edges, to our own lives. Some of us sniffle. Others of us sneer. For a moment, however, snifflers and sneerers are joined by a common bond: we saw *that* production, *that* film, *that* play. The same thing affected us all and took us, for several hours, out of ourselves, just as the prologue promised. It was a journey worth making, and making over and over again.

The important thing is that, when we come back, we come back a little wiser for the journey there and back again that we can make — but that the tragic characters cannot.

• Because of the name of the play — it's *Romeo and Juliet*, not Romeo and Rosaline — we know that Romeo falls out of love with Rosaline and into love with Juliet. What clues in the play lead you to believe that Romeo's feelings for Rosaline are being "in love with love"? Do you think his love for Juliet is real? What about hers for him?

ROMEO TOLD BENVOLIO THAT HE WAS IN LOVE WITH A GIRL, ROSALINE, WHO DID NOT LOVE HIM.

BE RULED BY ME; FORGET TO THINK OF HER.

THOU CANST NOT TEACH ME TO FORGET.

• One of the saddest aspects of Juliet's life seems to be that everyone she cares about fails her in one way or another — her parents turn on her; her nurse urges her to a bigamous marriage to Paris; Friar Laurence tries to hurry her away to a convent after Romeo's suicide. If you were her friend, what advice would you give her?

• Granted, we're reading a play by a Renaissance author about Renaissance Italy, and some of the values are different from our own. As ruler of Verona, Escalus has the right of life or death over his subjects. Do you think he handled the feud between the Montagues and the Capulets effectively? If you'd been his advisor, what would you have advised him to do?

• Do you see a difference in the values of the adults in this play and the young people?

MY EARS HAVE YET NOT DRUNK A HUNDRED WORDS OF THAT TONGUE'S UTTERANCE, YET I KNOW THE SOUND. ART THOU NOT ROMEO AND A MONTAGUE?

NEITHER, FAIR MAID, IF EITHER THEE DISLIKE.

• As you go through the play or this illustrated version, you'll see many references to the stars, to being star-crossed, to destiny. Do you think that Romeo and Juliet ever had a real chance for long-lasting happiness?

• In some early — and not particularly good — productions of Romeo and Juliet, the play is changed so that Juliet wakes up in time. Do you think this spoils things? Why or why not?

• After all is said and done, do you think Romeo and Juliet's life and death were worth it? Can you find things in the play — and in the principal characters — that you can relate to your own life?

ESSAYIST

Susan Shwartz, holds a B.A. from Mount Holyoke, and an M.A. and Ph.D. from Harvard University, and studied at Trinity College, Oxford. She is the author of *Cross and Crescent* (forthcoming from Tor Books); *Shards of Empire*; *Sisters in Fantasy II* ; *The Grail of Hearts* (which was nominated for Mythopoeic Society's Aslan Award); *Blood Feuds* (co-author; Baen 1993); *Blood Vengeance*; *Empire of the Eagle* , and other titles. Dr. Shwartz has taught at Ithaca College and Harvard University.